THIS QUIZ BOOK IS A GIFT

FROM: _______________________________

TO: _______________________________

DATE: _______________________________

RETURNING DATE: _______________________________

A LITTLE TRIP INSIDE YOU

WHAT'S YOUR FAVORITE BOOK?

# WHAT QUALITIES DO YOU ADMIRE ABOUT YOUR PARENTS?

# WHAT MAKES YOU FEEL MOST ALIVE?

IF YOU COULD HAVE ANYBODY ELSE'S LIFE,
WHO'S WOULD YOU TAKE?

IF YOU'RE HAVING A BAD DAY, HOW CAN I
CHEER YOU UP?

TAKE YOUR
TIME

# WHAT'S ONE THING THAT BOTHERS YOU MOST ABOUT THE WORLD TODAY?

# WHAT'S THE ONE THING YOU WOULD LIKE TO CHANGE ABOUT YOURSELF?

WHAT ACCOMPLISHMENT ARE YOU MOST
PROUD OF?

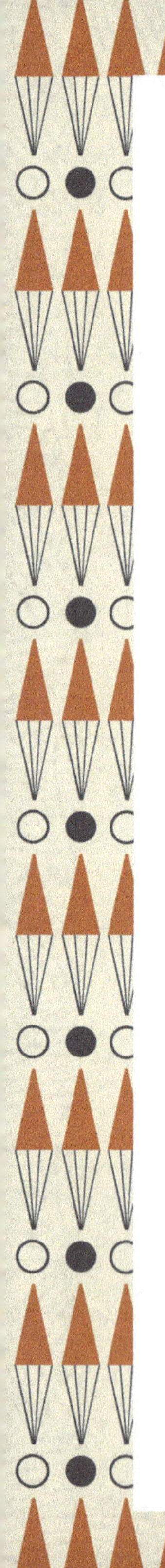

IF YOU ARE IN A BAD MOOD, DO YOU PREFER TO BE LEFT ALONE OR HAVE SOMEONE TO CHEER YOU UP?

HOW WOULD YOU DESCRIBE YOURSELF IN A SINGLE WORD?

HOW WOULD YOU DESCRIBE ME IN A SINGLE WORD?

DO YOU CRY AT MOVIES?

# THE SOUNDTRACK OF YOUR LIFE

ARE YOU A DOG PERSON OR A CAT PERSON?

DO YOU EVER DANCE EVEN IF THERE'S NO
MUSIC PLAYING?

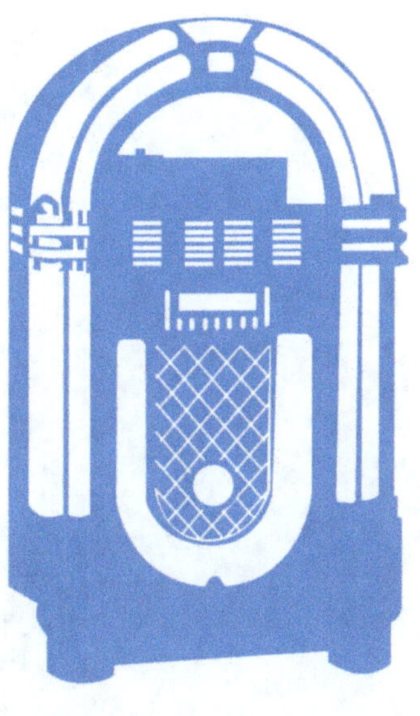

# WHAT ARE SOME OF YOUR FAVORITE CHILDHOOD MEMORIES?

IF YOU FOUND OUT TODAY WAS YOUR LAST
DAY ON EARTH, WHAT WOULD YOU WISH
YOU HAD DONE?

HOW WOULD YOU DRAW ME?

ALWAYS ON
THE ROAD

# WHAT IS ONE DREAM YOU HAVE YET TO ACCOMPLISH?

IF YOU HAD THE ABILITY TO ERASE SOMETHING
THAT YOU DID IN THE PAST, WHAT
WOULD IT BE?

# WHAT IS YOUR FIRST MEMORY?

# WHAT MAKES YOU FEEL LIKE YOU NEED TO BE ALONE?

# WHAT IS YOUR BIGGEST FEAR?

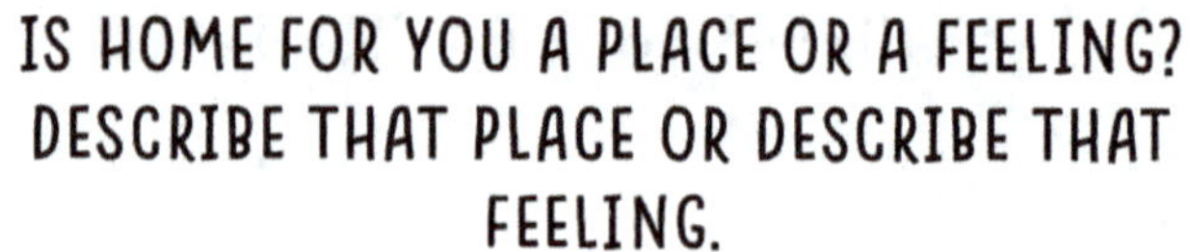


IS HOME FOR YOU A PLACE OR A FEELING?
DESCRIBE THAT PLACE OR DESCRIBE THAT
FEELING.

OPEN

WHERE'S ONE PLACE YOU'D LIKE TO GO THAT
YOU HAVEN'T BEEN?

WHAT FOOD COULD YOU NOT LIVE WITHOUT?

# WHO IS YOUR FAVORITE HISTORICAL FIGURE?

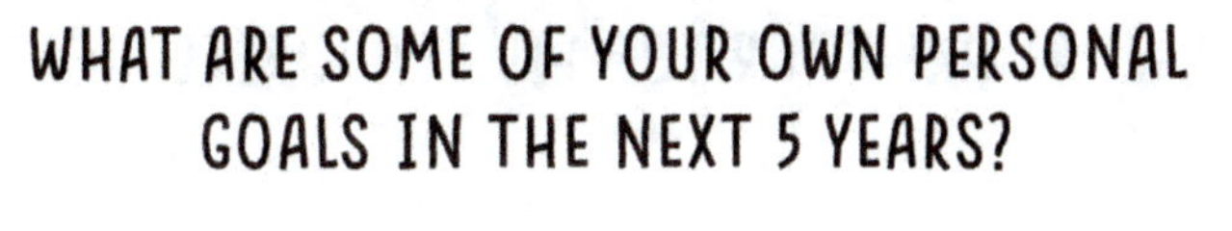

WHAT ARE SOME OF YOUR OWN PERSONAL
GOALS IN THE NEXT 5 YEARS?

# WHAT ARE YOUR TOP FIVE FAVORITE MOVIES?

# JUICY ANSWERS!

# WHAT'S SOMETHING I WOULD NEVER GUESS ABOUT YOU?

WHAT IS THE STRANGEST DREAM YOU'VE EVER HAD?

# WHAT SONG MAKES YOU UNCONDITIONALLY HAPPY?

# WHO IS YOUR GREATEST HERO?

WHAT'S AN IDEAL WEEKEND FOR YOU?

WHAT'S YOUR FAVORITE HOBBY TO DO ALONE?

# WHAT'S THE KINDEST THING SOMEONE'S DONE FOR YOU?

# SMILE!

# PRESENTED WITH THE OPPORTUNITY TO BE IMMORTAL WOULD YOU TAKE IT?

TELL ME A REALLY, REALLY STUPID JOKE THAT MADE YOU LAUGH.

# DID YOU EVER WRITE A JOURNAL?

WOULD YOU RATHER BE LOVED OR LOVE?

# HAVE YOU EVER LOST SOMEONE CLOSE TO YOU?

# WHAT MOVIE ARE YOU EMBARRASSED TO ADMIT YOU LOVE?

NO VACANCY
MOTEL
POOL
GO,
GO,
GO!

# WHAT WAS YOUR RELATIONSHIP LIKE WITH YOUR PARENTS?

# IF YOU COULD BE PRESIDENT OF YOUR COUNTRY FOR AN HOUR, WHAT IS THE ONE THING THAT YOU WOULD CHANGE?

# WHO ARE FIVE PEOPLE YOU ARE CLOSEST WITH?

# DO YOU HAVE ANY RECURRING DREAMS OR NIGHTMARES?

HOW DO YOU WISH TO BE REMEMBERED?

SUMMER
MEMORIES

# WHAT DID YOUR PAST RELATIONSHIP TEACH YOU?

# HAVE YOU EVER SEEN SOMETHING YOU CAN'T EXPLAIN?

## WHAT SCENE IN A MOVIE HAS EVOKED THE MOST FEELINGS OUT OF YOU?

# IF YOU COULD HAVE ANY SUPERHERO POWER, WHAT WOULD IT BE?

# WHAT SONG MAKES YOU UNCONDITIONALLY SAD?

IF LIFE
GIVE YOU
LEMONS...

DO YOU LIKE TO PLAN THINGS OUT OR DO YOU PREFER TO BE MORE SPONTANEOUS?

DO YOU LIKE TO SING IN THE SHOWER OR THE
CAR WHEN NO ONE IS AROUND?

# WHO WAS YOUR FAVORITE TEACHER AND WHY?

# WHAT'S THE CRAZIEST THING YOU'VE EVER DONE FOR LOVE?

# WHAT ARE YOUR TOP FIVE FAVORITE SONGS?

# WHICH ONE WOULD YOU DEDICATE TO ME?

YOU ARE
SO COOL

# IF YOU HAD THREE WISHES, WHAT WOULD THEY BE?

# WHAT ARE THREE THINGS YOU VALUE MOST ABOUT A PERSON?

WHAT DID YOU WANT TO BE WHEN YOU WERE
YOUNGER?

IF YOUR LIFE WAS A MOVIE OR A BOOK WHAT
WOULD BE THE TITLE TO IT?

WHAT ARE YOU MOST THANKFUL FOR?

# THE
# MAP OF
# YOUR LIFE

# WHAT'S YOUR DAY-TO-DAY MANTRA?

# IF YOU GOT A FREE CHEQUE FOR $5,000 RIGHT THIS SECOND, HOW WOULD YOU USE IT?

WHO IS THAT ONE PERSON YOU CAN TALK TO ABOUT JUST ANYTHING?
HI

WHERE IS YOUR FAVORITE PLACE IN THE
ENTIRE WORLD TO GO?

# WHAT WAS YOUR FIRST IMPRESSION OF ME?

YOU FINISHED IT!
NOW WRITE OR DRAW ANYTHING YOU WANT!

# CONGRATULATIONS!

YOU EARNED IT!